Frogs, Hogs, Puppy Dogs
Funny Children's Poems About Animal Friends

Poems by Leslie C. Halpern

Illustrations by Oral Nussbaum

Early Reader Ages 5-9

Cricket Cottage Publishing

I0098728

Copyright © 2014 Leslie C. Halpern. Illustrations copyright © 2014 Oral Nussbaum.

For information about group sales and permission, contact Cricket Cottage Publishing, LLC, 4409 Hoffner Avenue, Suite 127, Orlando, Florida 32812 or call 407-255-7785.

All rights reserved. No part of this work may be reproduced or transmitted in any form or by any means, electronic or otherwise, including photocopying and recording, or by any information storage or retrieval system, except as may be expressly permitted by the 1976 Copyright Act or in writing by the publisher.

ISBN: 978-0692258996
ISBN-10: 069225899X

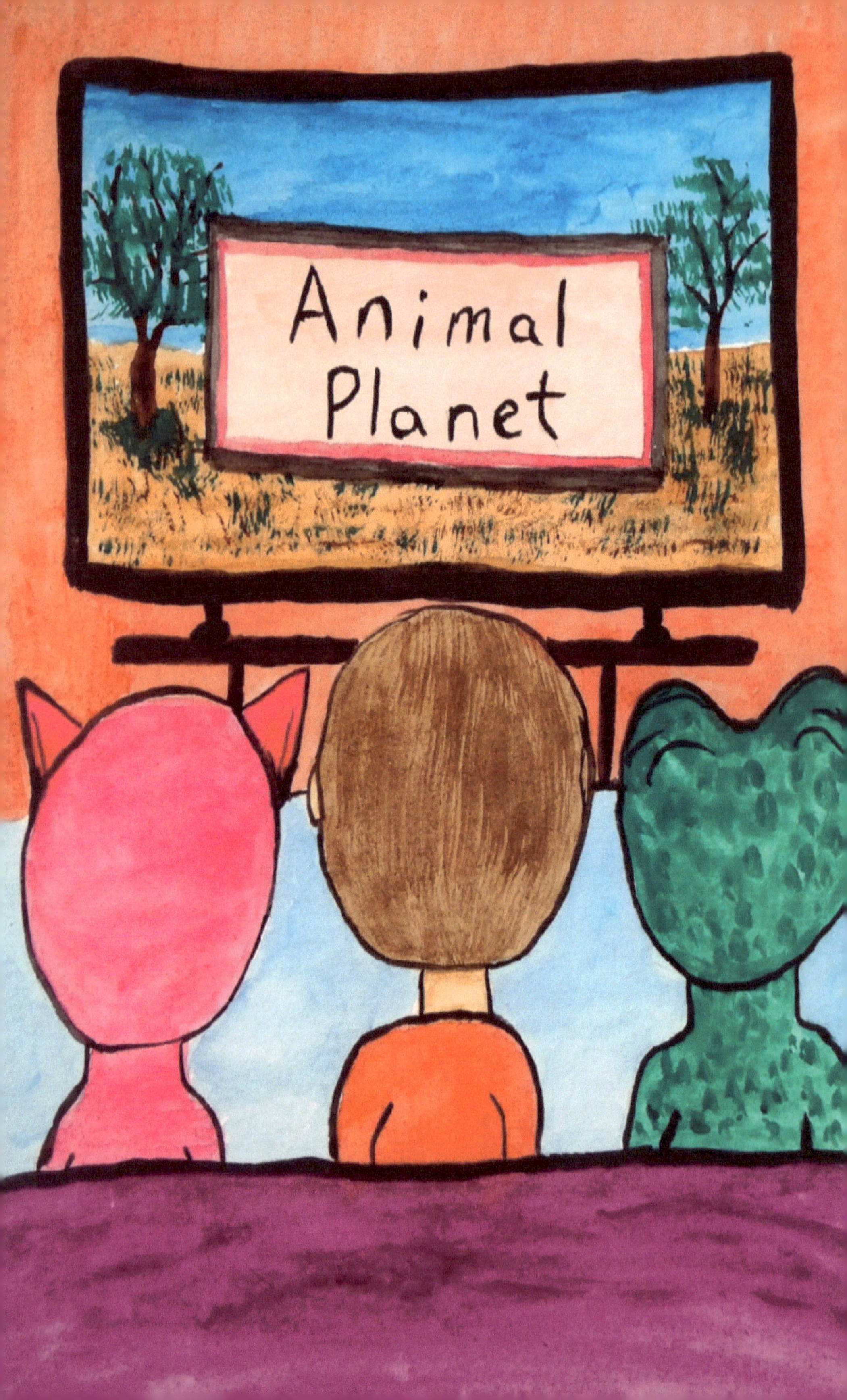
Animal
Planet

Child's Play

Small dogs, large hogs,
Frisbees to fetch.
Jumping toads, hopping frogs,
playing throw and catch.

Light brights, skin tights,
music, roll and rock 'em.
Bed springs, pillow fights,
football, try to block 'em.

Slip, slide, run, hide.
Tape, CD, and video.
Cakes, pies, food deep-fried.
It's fun to be a kideo.

Almost Everything

I love most things about my dog.
She's the greatest pet, I think.
I love her from her waggling tail
to her tiny tongue that's pink.

I love to watch her run and play,
scratch her itches, eat and drink.
I love her yippy little bark,
but don't like her doggone stink.

Frog Legs

I saw a frog on a log,
hopping frantically.
His legs were long.
He sang a song
a little bit off key.

"Ribbit Ow! Ribbit Ow!"
disturbed the quiet winter.
"Please help me now,
I'll show you how.
My left foot has a splinter."

With a shout, I pulled it out,
so that his pain would stop.
He looked at me --
walked naturally,
then said, "That's why frogs hop."

Squawk of the Town

I saw a real duck at the lake
while my family was out walking.
It was eating scraps of bread
while honking and squawking.

It tried to bite people's hands,
while it flapped its ugly feet.
That's the day when I learned
only rubber ducks are sweet.

The Shot

I took my pet
to the vet.

Unhappy Spot
got a shot

close to her thigh,
made her cry.

Her spirit sagged,
then tail wagged.

My happy Spot
soon forgot.

Zoo Life

Animals have
longer lives in zoos.
My teacher shared
this happy news.

They are hunted
in the wild,
and must find food
to feed their child.

There's no doctor
to cure their sickness.
It's called
survival of the fittest.

But in zoos
they get food and care
so it's good that
many types live there.

I'm glad zoo animals
live long because
it means there will
be more grand-paws.

Fleas

My little doggie has some fleas
on his belly, ears, and knees

above his whiskers, near his eyes
on his tail, around his thighs

on his paws, his back, his head
and since last night, they're in my bed.

Tanks A Lot

My goldfish swims in circles.
There isn't much to do.
If you were a goldfish,
I bet you'd just swim, too.

My Mom bought my first fish,
so I have her to thank.
I love to watch it swim around,
but don't like to clean the tank.

Silly Animal Names

Piglet is the name for a small pig.
Hogs are the name when they're really big.

So why aren't puppies called "doglets"
and baby frogs known as "froglets"?

Why can't we say small cats are "catlets"
and just call the baby bats "batlets"?

Baby frogs are known as "tadpoles"
and "pups" are young sharks, bats, and moles.

And I am also wondering
why a young fish is a "fingerling."

Baby kangaroos are called "joeys"
whether they are girls or boys.

"Chicks," "calves," "cubs" – it's too confusing.
There's just one name we should be using:

Let's all do what the mama goat did.
She calls her little kid a "kid."

Pretty Polly

My parrot has low self-esteem.
I'll tell you just what I mean.

Instead of trying to copy talk,
Polly will grunt, moan, and squawk.

She doesn't fly, just mopes around
with her beak pointed toward the ground.

She won't peck at her seeds for dinner,
but plucks out feathers to look thinner.

I've told her twice, but she hasn't heard:
Polly's already the perfect bird.

Bone
sweet
Bone

The Sunny Spot

I like the way my little dog
sleeps in the sunny spot.
When home is dark and wintry cold,
she'll find the place that's hot.

A tiny sliver of sunshine
is all that needs to please
my furry little friend as she
recharges batteries.

My Turtle

I have a turtle –
named him Groucho.

He likes to climb up
on the couch-o.

I feed him from a
little pouch-o.

One day he bit me.
Mucho oucho!

And that is why
he's called Groucho.

Snakes on a Bus

Kevin brought three snakes on the bus, bus, bus.
And waved them around at us, us, us.

The snakes stared, but didn't hiss, hiss, hiss.
Kevin screamed: "Take this, this, this!"

The driver slammed his brakes, brakes, brakes.
But Kevin's snakes were fakes, fakes, fakes.

Although the drive to school is far, far, far,
Kevin now must come by car, car, car.

Stray Cat

The little kitten was a stray.
I brought some milk, begged her to stay.
But then one day she ran away
to find another place to play.

A year later, there she sat
on my porch, a full-grown cat
asleep on top the welcome mat.
My cat came back, imagine that!

I saved her bed, bowl, scratching post —
all the things she loved the most.
I offered her sardines on toast
because I'm such a gracious host.

Squeaker of the House

I dress my dog in baby clothes,
clean her teeth and floss.
I rub a tissue on her nose
And brush her fur to gloss.

I cook her meals, make sure she's fed,
put ribbons in her hair
paint her nails fire engine red –
give tender loving care.

She has designer squeaky toys,
a padded stroller when we walk.
Her life is filled with countless joys.
I've started teaching her to talk.

Nutty Squirrel

Cartoon squirrels
are cute and sweet,
storing nuts
so they can eat.

Outside my house
high in the tree
nutty squirrel
just screeched at me.

He must need me
to go away.
I just wanted
to watch him play.

He won't perform
with his bad mood.
He only wants
to store his food.

Fussy Eater

My puppy will eat stickers,
postage stamps, letters, labels,
cardboard boxes, paper bags,
and things on kitchen tables.

Everything goes in her mouth.
She will swallow it down whole.
The only food she doesn't like
is whatever's in her bowl.

Trick
or
Tweet

Black Cats

Black cats are unlucky.
I hope our paths don't cross.
But if they do, I promise you
I'll let them know who's boss.

White cats, spotted cats
are mostly what I've seen.
Except one night a year;
black cats like Halloween.

Car Ride

The backseat makes me sleepy.
I try to stay awake.
Missing out on all the fun
would be a big mistake.

I listen to the radio --
count each Ford and Chevy,
but when we leave the neighborhood
my eyelids get too heavy.

They droop lower and lower
till eventually they close.
My mouth falls open, drool slips down,
and a snore comes out my nose.

I'm a very good sleeper,
in fact, I couldn't be prouder.
My dog's snore makes lots of noise,
but mine is even louder.

Hogs and Mufflers

A motorcycle's called a hog.
They both go very fast.
A hog grunts as it jogs.
The bike snorts out exhaust.

Bikes need gasoline for fuel.
Pig and hogs eat truffles.
I think it should be a law
that all hogs must have mufflers.

Learn More About Animal Friends

Does your family have a pet? Certain kinds of animals make better pets than others. One out of three homes in America has a dog, making dogs the most popular pet. Cats are the second most popular pet in the United States. How many poems can you find in this book that talk about dogs and cats?

♦ Most dogs love to chew on bones. Large raw bones are usually healthy for dogs to eat, but cooked bones sometimes splinter and can cause medical problems. Ask a veterinarian which bones are safe for your dog. Can you find all seven bones hidden in the pictures of this book?

♦ Sometimes the way we think about animals is different from the way they really are. A cartoon, movie, or video game can make animals seem much nicer or cuter than they are in real life. Can you find three poems in this book that show another side of animals (hints: one animal likes ponds and lakes; one animal eats flies and bugs; and one animal climbs trees).

♦ The poem "Zoo Life" talks about how animals live longer lives in zoos. They live longer there because they get medical care and have regular feeding times. Even so, many people argue that all animals should be free and live in their natural homes, such as jungles, deserts, forests, and oceans, rather than in man-made places like zoos. What do you think is best for animals? Why do you think this?

Learn New Words

Look for these words throughout the book. Sometimes words can have other meanings when used in different ways. This is what they mean in the poems in this book.

yippy: short, sharp noises made by a small animal
doggone: describing something that bothers you
frantically: wild with fear, pain, or excitement
splinter: a small, thin, sharp piece broken off from a larger piece
survival of the fittest: stronger, healthier animals live longer than weaker, less-healthy animals
sardines: a small oily fish eaten all over the world
gracious: kind and pleasant
Chevy: a nickname for Chevrolet, a popular car maker
eventually: at some later time
exhaust: waste gases coming from an engine or machine
truffles: a stinky underground fungus that pigs can smell
mufflers: (two different meanings) 1) a scarf worn around the neck for warmth; 2) part of a motor's exhaust system that quiets sound

If "Frogs, Hogs, Puppy Dogs" contains other words you don't know, try to figure out their meanings by how they are used. Then check the dictionary or ask an adult to see if you guessed right.

www.ingramcontent.com/pod-product-compliance
Lightning Source LLC
Chambersburg PA
CBHW041759040426
42447CB00001B/15

* 9 7 8 0 6 9 2 2 5 8 9 9 6 *